OUR • WORLD • MY • ROOTS

SOUTH AFRICA

WRITTEN BY ANNA MAKANDA & SHARMANE BARRETT

ILLUSTRATED BY ROSIE EDWARDS

OUR DEDICATIONS

In Anna's words:

To my parents, for always believing in me and encouraging me to shoot for the moon. To my mum, for teaching me that in order to know who you are, you must know where you come from. To my husband, for being my absolute rock through thick and thin. To my two beautiful children, who inspire me every day.

In Sharmane's words:

To my parents and my sisters for being my biggest challengers, as well as supporters, in life. To my ten amazing nieces and nephews, for being my constant reminder that I need to be a better me for all of the little eyes that are watching.

To all the little explorers,
may you always remember to:

BE CURIOUS

BE CONFIDENT

BE KIND

BE YOU

CONTENTS

NORTH AMERICA

EUROPE

AFRICA

SOUTH AFRICA

SOUTH AMERICA

ANTARCTICA

LOCATION

South Africa is a country at the southernmost tip of Africa. Its coast borders both the Atlantic Ocean and the Indian Ocean. It shares a land border with six countries. Namibia, Botswana, and Zimbabwe are to the north, Mozambique and Eswatini are to the east, and Lesotho is a small country in the middle, completely surrounded by South Africa.

Size: 471,445 mi²

Capital: South Africa has three capital cities: 🔍 Pretoria (the administrative capital), Bloemfontein (the judicial capital) and Cape Town (the legislative capital).

Currency: South African rand (ZAR)

Population: 60.9 million (2024)

Major Cities: Johannesburg, Cape Town, Durban, Pretoria, and Port Elizabeth 🔍

Highest Point: Mafadi peak, at 3,450 m

WEATHER

South Africa has four distinct seasons: summer (December to February), fall (March to May), winter (June to August), and spring (September to November). Due to the elevation above sea level, the temperatures are lower than in other surrounding countries. The average summer temperature is below 80 degrees Fahrenheit and in the winter, temperatures can drop below freezing.

LANGUAGES

South Africa has 12 official languages, reflecting its diverse cultural heritage. These languages include isiZulu, isiXhosa, Afrikaans, English, Sepedi, Setswana, Sesotho, Xitsonga, siSwati, Tshivenda, isiNdebele, and South African Sign Language.

RELIGION

Over 85% of South Africans are Christian. The remaining 15% practice other faiths including Islam, Hinduism, other traditional African religions and Judaism. More and more people today identify as agnostic or atheist.

PRETOR[I]

JOHANNESBURG

CONSTITUTION
HILL

BLOEMFONTEIN

MAFAD
MOUNTA[IN]

ORANGE RIVER

THE GREAT
ESCARPMENT

ROBBEN
ISLAND

CAPE
TOWN

GQEBERHA

BOULDERS
BEACH

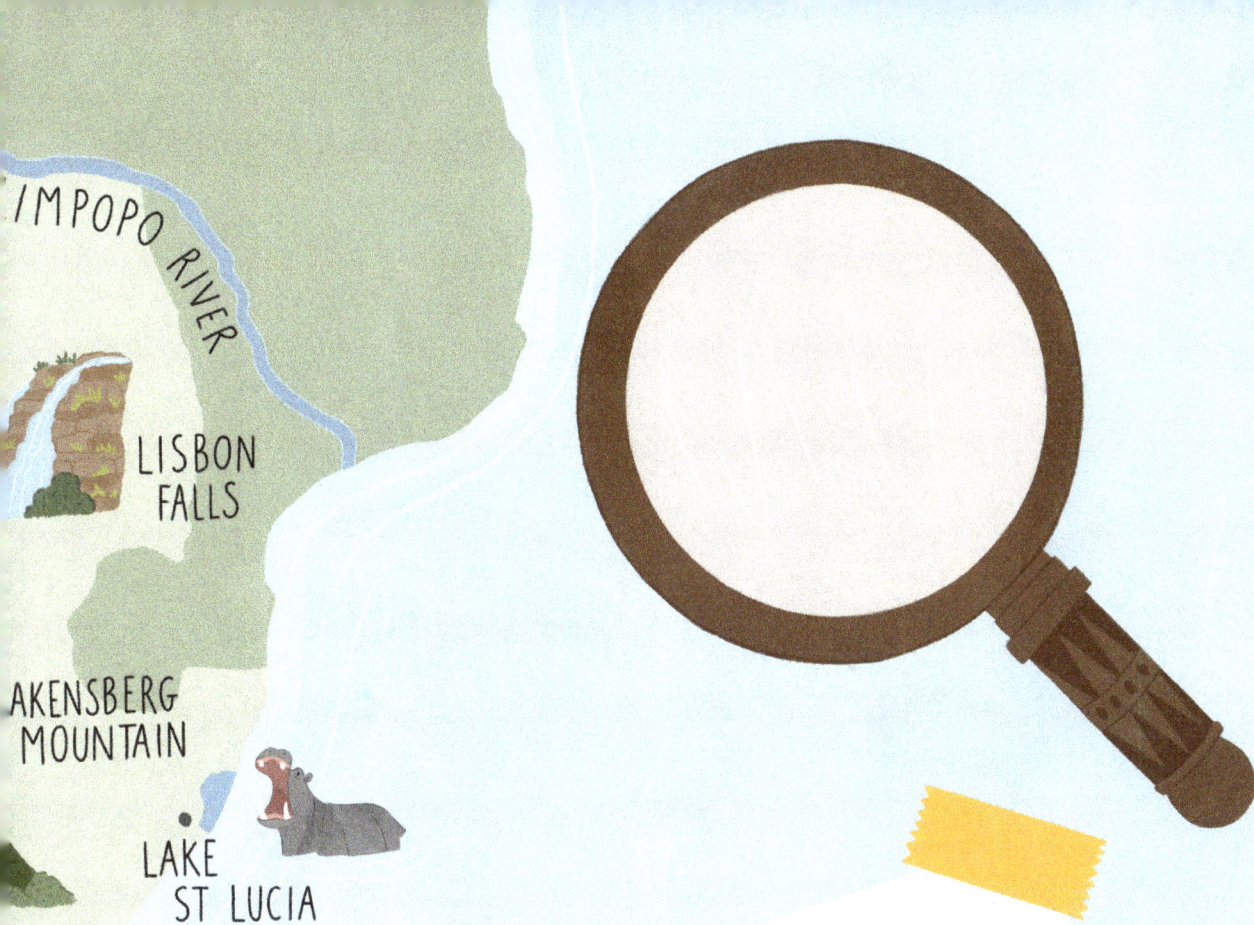

IMPOPO RIVER

LISBON
FALLS

AKENSBERG
MOUNTAIN

LAKE
ST LUCIA

URBAN

KEEP AN EYE OUT FOR

- Capital: Pretoria, Bloemfontein, Cape Town
- Major Cities: Johannesburg, Durban, Pretoria
- Mountains: Drakensberg Mountain Range
- Rivers: Orange, Limpopo
- Waterfalls: Lisbon Falls, Elands River Falls, Tugela Falls
- The Great Escarpment
- Nelson Mandela Square
- Soweto
- Boulders Bay

ARE YOU EXCITED ABOUT GOING ON AN ADVENTURE?

Join us on a journey across land and sea, transporting you to South Africa, known as the "Rainbow Nation": a land of many cultures, stunning landscapes, and rich history. From the majestic peaks of the Drakensberg Mountains to the vibrant bustle of its cities, South Africa offers a tapestry of experiences waiting to be explored. This book will guide you through the country's geography, people, culture, and beyond.

But there's more there than meets the eye: South Africa has an array of languages, communities, beliefs, and traditions. Despite its troubled history, the country remains vibrant and warm. The people of South Africa are known for their resilience, hospitality, and strong sense of identity.

You might be surprised to discover the similarities between South Africa and your own home, though lots of things are different, too.

South Africa is about eight times smaller than the United States, and home to over 60 million people who speak many languages.

Perhaps you have South African heritage and you want to learn more about your roots, or you simply wish to delve into the wonders of this remarkable country. You will see a glimpse into South Africa's unique charm, but there is much more to uncover beyond these pages. We hope that someday you will be able to travel all the way to South Africa and beyond.

THERE ARE 12 OFFICIAL LANGUAGES SPOKEN IN SOUTH AFRICA.

Here is how to say "Hello" in five languages.

GOEIEDAG
(AFRIKAANS)

DUMELA
(SEPEDI)

HELLO

In many South African cultures, traditional greetings involve more than just a simple handshake. For example, in the Zulu culture, people may greet each other with a handshake followed by a slight bow or nod along with the traditional greeting "Sawubona" (hello), "Unjani" (how are you?), while in the Xhosa culture, a handshake may be accompanied by a traditional greeting such as "Molo" (hello), "Unjani" (how are you?).

MOLO
(ISIXHOSA)

SAWUBONA
(ISIZULU)

Throughout the pages of this book you will find many words and phrases translated in:
isiZulu (blue)
isiXhosa (red)

HI, WELCOME TO SOUTH AFRICA.

MY NAME IS LERATO AND
I AM 7 YEARS OLD.

THIS IS MY YOUNGER SISTER,
KAYA. SHE IS 5 YEARS OLD.

AND THIS IS MY BEST FRIEND,
THABO (SHORT FOR LETHABO).
HE IS THE SAME AGE AS ME.

WE ARE REALLY EXCITED TO SHOW
YOU AROUND...

LET'S BEGIN OUR ADVENTURE!

MEET MY FAMILY

I live with Kaya, our two big brothers – Langa and Lwazi – Mom, Dad, and our grandparents. We speak isiZulu and English. I have lots of aunts, uncles, and cousins too. Let me introduce you to my...

Family
Umndeni Usapho

Mom
Umama Umama

Dad
Ubaba Utata

Sister
Udadewethu Usisi

Brother
Umfowethu Ubhuti

Grandad
Umkhulu Utatomkhulu

Grandma
Ugogo Umakhulu

Uncle
Umalume Umalume

Auntie
Umalumekazi Umakazi

Cousin
Umzala Umzala

Cousin
Umzala Umzala

Friend
Umngani Umhlobo

Friend
Umngani Umhlobo

11

THABO'S FAMILY LIVE IN THE NEIGHBORHOOD.

They speak isiXhosa and English. We call adults "Meneer," "Mevrou," or "Juffrou" (Mr, Mrs, or Miss). This is the respectful way to speak to grown-ups.

DID YOU KNOW?

In many South African cultures, when a baby is given their name, it comes with a big celebration known as a naming ceremony. The name is a way for families to honor their heritage, connecting the child to their ancestors.

Lerato means "Love"
Kaya means "Restful place"
Thabo means "Happiness"

WHERE WE LIVE

The Khoikhoi and San people were the original inhabitants of Southern Africa. The KohiSan (Bushmen) today are nomads who live in the desert region. Many South Africans have left their traditional villages and now live in the cities and towns. The Z people are the largest ethnic group in South Africa; many still live in Kwazulu Natal, in the north eastern region of the country.

Between 1948 and 1994, people had to live in separate areas according to the color of their skin. Many townships were built for black people and other non-white people. This period was called apartheid. Today, people can choose where they live.

Home
Ikhaya Ekhaya

Kaya and I both live in a house in Soweto, Johannesburg. Thabo lives with his family on the same street. Soweto is a melting pot of South African cultures.

My cousins Bongi and Solomon live in a house in Khayelitsha, Cape Town.

Uncle Siphiwe lives in an apartment in Pretoria. When he visits, he tells us stories about his travels across the country for meetings. He especially likes to visit Stellenbosch; we love to hear him describe the beautiful big houses there.

DID YOU KNOW?

South Africa has one of the largest populations of African countries below the equator, but its landmass covers only 4% of the entire African continent.

14

LET'S EXPLORE

LANDSCAPES

Kaya and I would love to explore more of South Africa. We are not able to travel very much but we have taken two trips. Umama and Ubaba take us on the bus. It is such an adventure. One day we would like to go on the train. Here are some of the things we would like to see...

Explore
Hlola Ukuhlola

MOUNTAINS Q

South Africa has over 60 mountain ranges, with some of the country's highest peaks in the Drakensberg Mountain range (Dragon's mountain). These include:

Mafadi

Champagne Castle

Popple

16

LAKES

South Africa is home to more than 50 lakes, including Lake St. Lucia and Lake Sibhayi. Lake St. Lucia is a UNESCO World Heritage Site and provides a life source for diverse wildlife, including hippos and crocodiles. Most of South Africa's lakes were made by building dams.

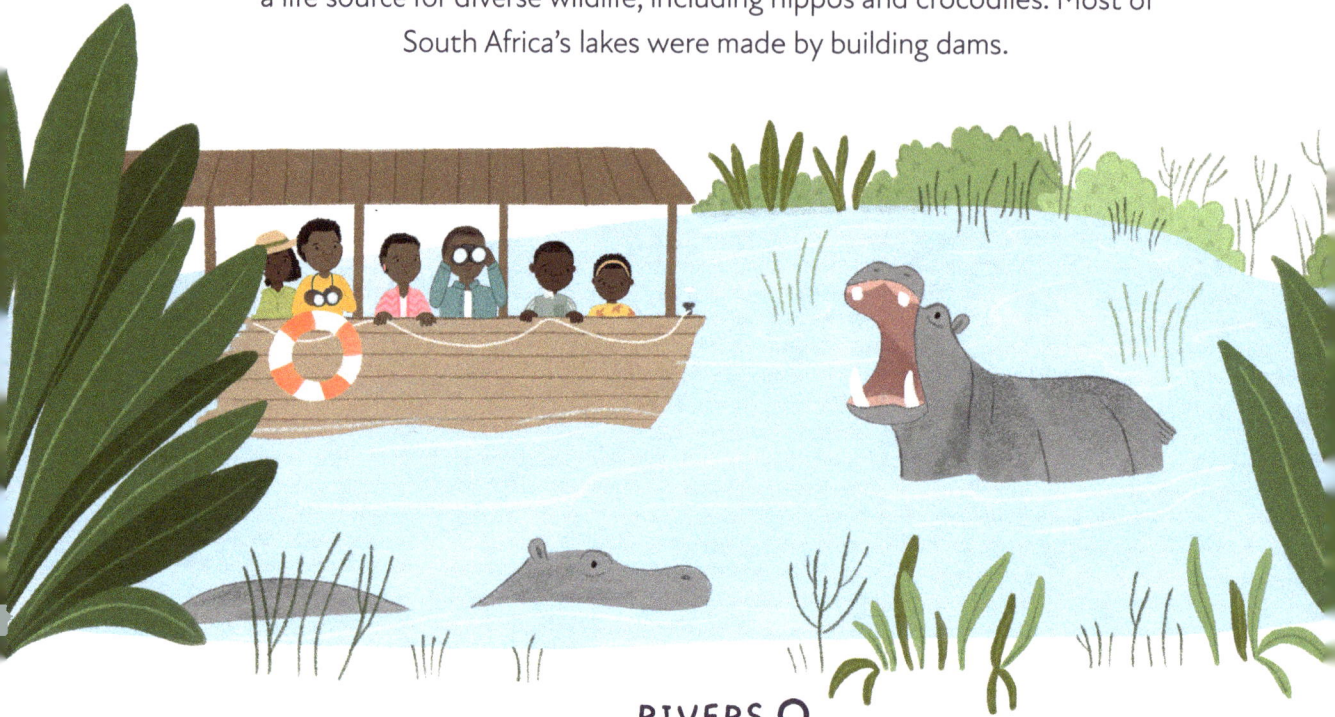

RIVERS Q

There are over 20 major rivers in South Africa, but two of the most prominent are:

The Orange River, which is the longest river in South Africa. It starts in the Drakensberg Mountain range and flows westward into the Atlantic Ocean through Alexander Bay.

Q: How many crocodiles long is the Orange River?
A: 540,444 crocodiles long – approximately 1,511 m

The Limpopo River, which forms part of South Africa's northern border with Botswana and Zimbabwe. It flows eastward into the Indian Ocean.

Q: How many crocodiles long is the Limpopo River?
A: 388,888 crocodiles long – approximately 1,087 m

WATERFALLS 🔍

There are 25 breathtaking waterfalls in South Africa, including Elands River Falls, Tugela Falls and the highest and most dramatic of the falls, Lisbon Falls.

Elands River Falls

Tugela Falls

DID YOU KNOW?

South Africa is the only country that borders both the Indian and Atlantic Oceans. The point at which they meet is the southernmost tip of Africa.

THE GREAT ESCARPMENT ◎

The great escarpment is a large formation which extends across the borders of South Africa, into Zimbabwe, Mozambique, Namibia, and Angola. An escarpment is a steep slope that separates two areas of land at different heights. It was formed around 180 million years ago, when the earth's continental crust expanded.

SAVANNAS

The savannas are wide stretches of grasslands, known for having scattered trees and a lot of wildlife. They cover more than a third of the country, providing a home for animals like cheetahs, jackals, and wildebeest. There are also over 5,700 types of plants and trees found on South Africa's savannas.

FORESTS

South Africa is home to a variety of forests, including the Knysna Forest and the Tsitsikamma Forest. These forests are full of a diversity of flora and fauna, including native trees like yellowwood and stinkwood. Most of South Africa's forests are managed as conservation areas.

DESERTS

There are three deserts in South Africa. The Karoo desert, and parts of the Kalahari and the Namib deserts.

THE CENTRAL PLATEAU

The Central Plateau is a high flat area which dominates South Africa's landscape. This area is surrounded by coastal lowlands and the Great Escarpment on its outer edge.

BUSHVELD

The bushveld is a thornbush field with trees, thorn bushes and tall grass. It is found in Limpopo, and extends into northern KwaZulu-Natal province, Swaziland, Mozambique, Zimbabwe, and Botswana.

COASTLINE

South Africa has a long coastline stretching more than 3,000 km from the desert border with Namibia on the Atlantic Ocean, around the tip of Africa and then north to the border of Mozambique on the Indian Ocean.

DID YOU KNOW?

More than 2,000 shipwrecks lie under the waters off the coastline of South Africa; it used to be the main trading route from Europe to India, known as "the spice route."

PLANTS AND TREES

South Africa has a varied climate and geography which means that there are many different plants and trees. Some of South Africa's most important trees are the Baobab, Acacia, Sausage Tree, Aloe Vera, Spekboom and the Cape Floral Kingdom (which is Kaya's favorite as it sounds like a magical faraway world!).

We have so much fun climbing trees. One time, Thabo and I wanted to see who could climb the highest. We got so carried away we forgot we also had to get back down. When we couldn't climb any higher we got stuck and had to wait for Ubaba to come to rescue us!

Baobab

Aloe Vera

Sausage Tree

Tree
Isihlahla Umthi

DID YOU KNOW?

A sausage tree grows a poisonous fruit that is up to 60 cm long, weighs about 7 kg and looks like a sausage in a casing. Its leaves can be used to help treat snake bites.

FACTS

The real yellowwood tree is one of South Africa's most iconic trees, it is also the national tree of South Africa. It can live for over 1,000 years, grow up to 40 metres in height (in the forest) and it is thick with glossy, dark evergreen leaves.

The ripe berry-like cones are eaten by birds, monkeys, bushpigs and sometimes people.

A lot of people say the real yellowwood is beautiful, and its wood comes in a soft yellow color.

THE KING PROTEA
(THE NATIONAL FLOWER)

This unique flower is known for its striking appearance: large, showy blossoms with prominent, feathery petals surrounding a central cone. It is also known as the sugarbush or the cape artichoke flower. The king protea is not just a flower. The leaves can be enjoyed in tea, and the nectar from the flowers has traditionally been used as medicine.

The king protea is native to South Africa and it is a symbol of the tough and resilient spirit of the country. The national cricket team is named after it.

HERE ARE SOME OF THE MANY OTHER ANIMALS AND AMPHIBIANS YOU MAY FIND IN SOUTH AFRICA. SEE IF YOU CAN SPOT THEM:

African Elephant, Lion, Leopard, Cape Buffalo, Rhinoceros, Cheetah, Giraffe, Hippopotamus, African Penguin, Knysna Seahorse (Hippocampus capensis), De Winton's Golden Mole, Cape Golden Mole, Table Mountain Ghost Frog, Cape Grysbok, Cape Mountain Zebra, Aardvark, Tsessebe, Gemsbok, Greater Kudu Bull, Puff Adder, Springbok, Wildebeest, Golden Mole, Least Dwarf Shrew.

ANIMALS

Izilwane Izilwanyana

Ubaba says that one of the best things about South Africa is being able to see so many animals – they are so beautiful. He promised that one day he will take us all to Kruger National Park to see them in the wild.

DID YOU KNOW?

Golden Moles are almost extinct, but the only country in the world where they can still be found is South Africa.

26

TABLE MOUTAIN

Table mountain is one of the most popular tourist attractions in South Africa. It is a flat-topped mountain with breathtaking views of the city and the surrounding coastline. It ends at the Cape of Good Hope and Cape Point, which is at the southernmost tip of the Cape Peninsula. You can see panoramic views of the Atlantic Ocean and False Bay from this viewing point.

BOULDERS BAY PENGUIN COLONY 🔍

The main colony is on Foxy Beach, and it is one of only two land-based colonies in the world. If you're lucky, in the summer it is possible to go for a swim in the sea and be joined by some paddling penguins.

D
YOU KNOW

The sardine run
fish migration wh
takes place yearly in
waters off Cape Poin
is up to 15 km long, 3
wide and 40 m de
The sardine run
be seen fr
spa

ROBBEN ISLAND

From 1961, the island (off the coast of Cape Town) was used by the government as a maximum-security prison. The prison was closed in the 1990s, and it is now a museum and heritage site, because of its importance to the country's political history. Robben Island is best known for being the place where Nelson Mandela was imprisoned for 18 years during the apartheid era.

BLYDE RIVER CANYON

This is one of the largest canyons in the world, the best way to see it is to drive the Panorama Route which connects the three best viewpoints: Three Rondavels, God's Window and Bourke's Luck Potholes. Here you will see many cliffs, lush vegetation, and stunning plunge pools. Kaya and I can't wait to visit. You can do lots of activities there, including hiking, mountain biking, abseiling, hot air ballooning, whitewater rafting and horse riding.

28

JOHANNESBURG

Johannesburg, often referred to as "Joburg" or "Jozi," is the largest city in South Africa and one of the most vibrant cities in Africa. It is known as the "City of Gold." We love it when Ugogo and Umkhulu tell us stories of when they were growing up, and how different the city is today.

Some great places to see in Johannesburg are:

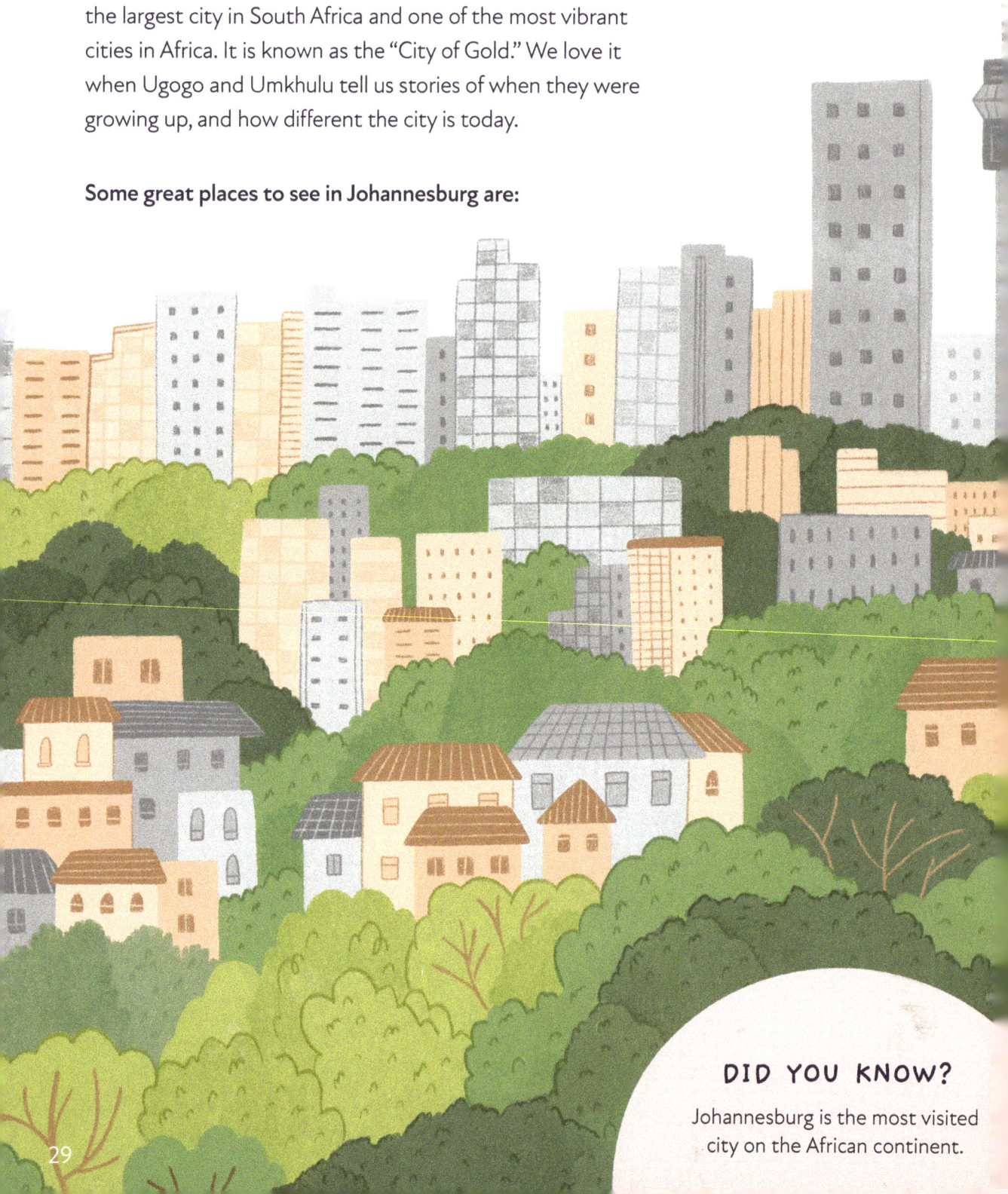

DID YOU KNOW?

Johannesburg is the most visited city on the African continent.

APARTHEID MUSEUM

The museum gives a view of the apartheid era through photos, interactive exhibits and artifacts.

CONSTITUTION HILL

Constitution Hill was once a prison. It is now a museum which shows the country's political journey. It is also home to the Constitutional Court of South Africa.

SOWETO 🔍

Soweto is the country's largest township, and now home to historical sites such as the Hector Pieterson Museum, and Vilakazi Street (the only street in the world where not just one, but two Nobel Peace Prize winners once lived). There are many local markets to visit where people shop for gifts, handcrafted goods and art, or fresh food and delicious treats.

NELSON MANDELA SQUARE 🔍

Ugogo and Umkhulu like to take us to see the statue of Nelson Mandela on the square. It's huge! They talk a lot about the important work he did when he was alive.

GOLD REEF CITY

Gold Reef City is a theme park built on an old gold mine. Umama says it looks like the old mining town during the Gold Rush Era. Thabo and I want to visit the theme park to go on all of the rides!

LET'S GO TO SCHOOL

Thabo and I go to the same school in Soweto. We are in grade two and Kaya is in the kindergarten class which is in the same building.

Our school is not very big, but it has ten classrooms. There is lots of space outdoors where we play sports and have fun at playtime. We learn in English and Zulu. Our teacher loves events and celebrations. My favorite is heritage day, where we all get to help make decorations for the classroom.

School

Isikole Isikolo

My cousins, Bongi and Solomon, go to school in the rural area of Gomoa District in Cape Coast. Every day, they have to walk a long way to and from school. Their school is much smaller, with only a few classrooms.

Student
Isitshudeni Umfundi

Teacher
Uthishela Utitshala

Homework
Umsebenzi wesikole
Umsebenzi wasekhaya

Lesson
Isifundo Isifundo

WE HAVE THE MOST FUN IN OUR...

MUSIC LESSONS
We play these instruments:

A MUSICAL
BOW

BASS
GUITAR

MARIMBA

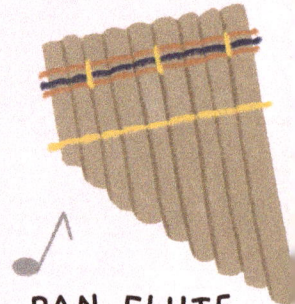

PAN FLUTE

There is also time for dancing. As soon
as the music starts, we can't help it.
We dance a lot!

PE LESSONS

At school we play soccer, athletics and netball.

Outside school, we play cricket and we like to swim.

DID YOU KNOW?

South Africa is best known for playing rugby, and the national team, the Springboks, has many passionate supporters. Rugby is a great sport because it brings people from different backgrounds together, both players and fans.

34

LET'S PLAY

**In the playground at school, one of
my favorite games to play is...**

Kgati
Players: 3+

Kgati (also known as jump rope)
Two players hold each end of the skipping rope and the third
player jumps the rope in different styles whilst chanting and
singing. The jumping player often shows off their tricks.

Sometimes we have three or four people jumping the rope at the same time – it's so much fun to see how long we can keep going before someone gets caught by the rope!

Thabo and I have jump rope competitions with our friends. We challenge each other to jump 100 times with legs together, 100 times with a single leg, 100 times with the other leg and finally 100 times on both hands and feet.

Play
Dlala Dlala

LET'S LEARN

NUMBERS
Inombolo Inani

I have been helping Kaya learn to write her numbers.

We can help you learn to count to ten.

1 KUNYE
NYE

2 KUBILI
MBINI

3 KUTHATHU
NTATHU

4 KUNE
NE

Learn
Funda Funda

5 KUHLANU
NTLANU

6 ISITHUPHA
NTANDATHU

7 ISIKHOMBISA
XHENXE

8 ISISHIYAGALOMBILI
SIBHOZO

9 ISISHIYAGALOLUNYE
LITHOBA

10 ISHUMI
SHUMI

38

THE ALPHABET
Incwadi Unobumba

Learning the alphabet is also fun.

How many letters can you say?

A EY
A

B BI
BA

C SI
CE

D DI
DI

E I
E

F EF
FO

G JI
GU

H ETSCH
HA

I AY
I

J JEY
JA

K KHEY
KU

L EL
LA

M EM
M

N EN
NA

O OW
O

P PHI
PI

Q QYU
QU

R AR
RA

S ES
SI

T THI
TE

U YU
U

V VI
VU

W DBLYU
WA

X EKS
XA

Y WAY
YI

Z ZETH
ZI

LET'S SAY

Here are some of our everyday words and phrases.
Why not try and say them?

HOW ARE YOU?

Unjani?

Unjani?

HOW OLD ARE YOU?

Uneminyaka emingaki?

Uneminyaka emingaphi?

MY NAME IS...

Igama lami ngu...

Igama lam ngu...

I AM ... YEARS OLD

Ngineminyaka engu...

Ndineminyaka e...

GOOD MORNING

Sawubona

Molo ngalentsasa

GOOD AFTERNOON

Sawubona

Molo Ngalenjikalanga

GOOD NIGHT

Ulale Kahle

Busuku benzolo

I LOVE YOU

Ngiyakuthanda

Ngiyakuthanda

THANK YOU

Ngiyabonga

Enkosi

PLEASE

Ngiyacela

Nceda

LET'S EAT
FOOD & DRINK

Eat
Yidla Yitya

Yummy
Kumnandii Mnandi

LERATO

I like to eat putu pap (cornmeal) for breakfast. My favorite dinner is bobotie, which is a curried meat casserole. Ugogo's bobotie is the best!

KAYA

I like it when Umkhulu cooks pap and wors for breakfast. Pap and wors is a maize porridge and boerewors is grilled sausage. Yum yum. My favorite dinner is chicken on the braai, which is a kind of barbecue.

THABO

I like to eat rusks for breakfast. It's a dried sweet bread. On the weekend, I have omelet.

My favorite dinner is bunny chow: a hollowed-out loaf of bread filled with curry, typically made with chicken, lamb, or vegetable curry. We eat it when we visit family in Kwazulu Natal.

There are so many delicious snacks that we all love:

Biltong: Dried and cured meat.

Samoosas: Triangular pastries filled with spicy meat.

Braaibroodjies: Grilled sandwiches made with cheese, tomato, and onion.

Koeksisters: Deep-fried dough infused with syrup, twisted into a braid-like shape, and coated in syrup or sugar.

Melktert: A traditional South African dessert consisting of a sweet pastry crust filled with creamy custard, flavored with cinnamon.

Droëwors: Similar to biltong, droëwors is a type of dried and cured sausage, but it's usually thicker and made from minced beef or game meat.

We also love to snack on fruit including: mango, marula fruit and star apples.

PUBLIC HOLIDAYS

We celebrate different public holidays in South Africa. Some are happy celebrations that represent a new beginning, others are to remember the country's journey, its struggles and wins. We have these days to honor important events and people. We have:

21st March-Human Rights Day—one of the most important public holidays in South Africa as it shines a light on the people who fought for all our rights by opposing apartheid. It also represents the ongoing struggle for equality in South Africa.

First Monday of April-Family Day—a day to celebrate family values and relationships, and for families to spend time with one another.

27th April-Freedom Day—a day to celebrate the first democratic elections held in South Africa in 1994, after apartheid.

1st May-Labour Day—recognized internationally as a day to celebrate workers.

16th June-Youth Day—commemorates the Soweto Uprising of 1976; a protest about education led by black school children, which resulted in a wave of protests across the country.

9th August-National Women's Day—a day to remember the 1956 Women's March to the Union Buildings in Pretoria, and women that fought in the struggle against apartheid.

24th September-Heritage Day—a day South Africans celebrate their diverse cultural heritage.

16th December-Day of Reconciliation—a day to recognize national unity and forgiveness among South Africans of all races and backgrounds.

26th December-Day of Goodwill—is traditionally a day to pack up the excess from Christmas Day to give to those in need.

We celebrate birthdays, Easter, Christmas, and New Year's Day. We also mark Mandela Day (July 18th) and Africa Day (May 25th).

LET'S CELEBRATE

We celebrate through a variety of cultural, traditional and religious events, as well as public holidays. These celebrations often involve vibrant music, dance, and communal gatherings. Family is very important, and gatherings with extended family members are common during holidays and special occasions.

CULTURAL FESTIVALS

Our festivals are a colorful blend of customs and rituals which are celebrated across the country, throughout the year. There is often a showcase of traditional music, dance, food, and art from different ethnic groups, allowing people to celebrate and learn about each other's cultures.

Celebrate
Ukugubha Bhiyoza

Party
Umcimbi Itheko

Merry Christmas
Ukhisimuzi Omuhle Krismesi emnandi

Happy Birthday
Jabulela Usuku Lokuzalwa
Mini Emnandi Yokuzalwa

Happy New Year
Jabulela Unyaka Omusha
Nyaka Omtsha Omyoli

CHRISTMAS

The festivities begin on Christmas Eve - we are excited every year; magic is in the air! Umkhulu really enjoys the carol singing and we often go to the candlelight services.

We get up early and go to a church service in the morning to reflect on the meaning of Christmas. As soon as we get home, we rush to open our gifts. Friends and family gather for lunch or dinner, followed by a game of cricket in the backyard.

We love to feast on Christmas day. It is a tradition for our whole family to sit in a circle and eat outside. There is always so much food to choose from: sometimes roast turkey, but often meat from the braai or Potjiekos (stew). We always have delicious desserts, including mince pies and the traditional Malva pudding which is sweet and sticky. I love it best when it is warm and Umama gives us an extra big scoop of ice cream.

When it gets dark, there are fireworks in the neighborhood. We LOVE to watch the sky light up with the colorful explosions. It is a special part of the day!

Today's culture in South Africa is a special blend of tradition and western culture, which you can see in the art, music and food.

GIVING GIFTS

Gifts are given for special occasions, celebrations or visiting someone's home. In more rural communities, they are typically items like school books, soap, candles or other practical items. Whether it's a small token of appreciation or otherwise, gift-giving plays a significant role in South African culture.

DRESSING UP

Most of the time, we wear the same kind of clothes that children wear in the UK, but Umama makes us dress smartly for church. Traditional clothing varies, depending on the ethnic group. There are a few well-known indigenous tribes that have shaped South African style, especially the Xhosa, Zulu and Ndebele tribes. Wearing cultural clothes is a way for us to show pride in our identity. The fabrics often have colorful beads, embroidery and patterns.

ART

The cave paintings discovered in South Africa are thought to be the oldest art objects in the world, dating back over 70,000 years. Nowadays, the country has a diverse range of contemporary artists.

DANCING

Dancing is a lifestyle, it is rooted in culture. People are strongly connected to music, and it is a celebration of the past and the present. There are many styles of dance including IsiPantsula, Bhenga, Gumboot and Indlamu. Dancing is a way for people to show their joy and unity as well as their sorrow and anger.

PLAYING MUSIC

Music is important to the majority of South Africans and when the music starts playing, everyone comes alive. At festivals, parties and cultural events we enjoy traditional music like kwaito, maskandi, gqom and gospel, as well as modern genres like afro-pop, hip-hop and amapiano.

EATING

Braaing (having a barbecue) is a popular tradition. It brings people together. Friends and family gather to grill meat, share stories, and enjoy each other's company. Weekends and special holidays are the best time to have a braai, and we sometimes do it at the beach.

LET'S GET LUCKY

What things bring you good luck or bad luck? Here are some of ours...

GOOD LUCK

Spotting a rainbow brings blessings and positive energy.

Wearing red underwear, especially on New Year's Eve, is believed
to bring good luck and prosperity for the coming year.

Eating black-eyed peas on New Year's Day is believed
to bring good luck and prosperity for the year ahead.

Dreaming about fish is believed to be a sign
of good luck and abundance.

Luck

Inhlanhla Ithamsanqa

BAD LUCK

Placing shoes on the table is considered unlucky as it is seen as disrespectful or inviting chaos.

Seeing a moonbow is believed to be a sign of impending disaster or misfortune.

Putting a hat on the bed is believed to bring bad luck; it is seen as disrupting the balance or inviting negative energy.

LET'S DREAM

Sometimes we close our eyes and dream about what we would like to be when we grow up.

Do you know what you would like to be?

Dream
Iphuphoi Iphupha

My favorite thing is to help other people. Ugogo talks about Nelson Mandela a lot, and when I grow up, I want to inspire people, just like him.

NELSON MANDELA

Nelson Mandela is often referred to as Madiba or Tata. He was an activist and philanthropist who became South Africa's first black president and a global symbol of peace. He became an important figure in fighting racial inequality during apartheid, for which he was arrested and spent 27 years in prison. He spent 67 years of his life fighting for equality and promoting peace.

I also enjoy making people laugh and so my friends often tell me I would make a great comedian like Trevor Noah.

TREVOR NOAH

Trevor is a comedian, writer, and award-winning television host best known for hosting a popular show in the USA. Trevor grew up in Soweto and his family were quite poor, but he has turned his childhood experiences into stories that make people laugh. He was a leading stand-up comedian in South Africa, before he found great success in the US. He is very vocal about wanting to help young people, and he started a foundation to help provide access to better education for young people in Joburg.

Thabo is also a fantastic rugby player and he loves to watch Siya Kolisi play.

SIYA KOLISI

Siya made history in 2018 when he became the Springboks' first black captain and led the team to victory at the Rugby World Cup in 2019. From the age of twelve he has won various scholarships, played for youth teams, and represented South Africa's national under 18s rugby union team. He founded the Kolisi Foundation, which was set up to help make opportunities fairer for the youth across South Africa.

Kaya is only five but she is quite a character. Umama says she can see her being a Hollywood actress like Charlize Theron...

CHARLIZE THERON

Charlize is an award-winning actress and producer, one of the most successful in Hollywood. She is also well known for the work she does for good causes. Her foundation supports communities in Southern African countries with health and education programmes. She helps programmes supporting women who are victims of violence.

Kaya is also obsessed with planes. It would be so cool if she were to become a fighter pilot like Mandisa Mfeka.

MANDISA MFEKA

Mandisa loved watching planes fly since she was five years old! She is the first black woman to be a Combat Fighter Pilot Major in South Africa and says it is like being the "police of the air." Mandisa volunteers for a charity that helps young girls progress in aviation, innovation and technology. Umama says she is paving the way for women and girls in aviation.

SALA
KAHLE
(ISIZULU)

GOODBYE

HAMBA
KAKUHLE
(ISIXHOSA)

National anthem

Nkosi Sikelel' iAfrika (God Bless Africa)

Iculo Lesizwe   Umhobe Wesizwe

MEANING OF THE FLAG

Black   The native people of South Africa

Green   The fertility of the land

Gold   The country's mineral wealth

Red   The bloodshed and sacrifices made
in the struggle for freedom and equality

White   Peace between the European and minority
populations of South Africa.

Blue   Opportunities for progress and prosperity;
the sky's the limit

DID YOU KNOW?

The same color combination is used
in the flags for Italy, Hungary, Monaco,
Indonesia and Sierra Leone.

HISTORY

c.73 000 BCE	Human paintings and artifacts in Blombos Cave
1000 BCE	The hunter-gatherer San and Khoikhoi tribes, commonly known as the Khoisan, inhabit Southern Africa
1480s	The Portuguese "discover" the southern tip of Africa
1652	Arrival of Dutch settlers marking the beginning of European colonization
1815	British sovereignty recognized at the Cape
1838	The Battle of Blood River
1867–1886	Goldrush era
1910	Union of South Africa formed
1948	The National Party (controlled by the Afrikaans) comes to power and apartheid begins
1960	Sharpeville demonstrations against apartheid
1976	The Soweto Uprising
1990	Apartheid activist Nelson Mandela is released from prison
1994	Nelson Mandela becomes the country's first black president, and the end of apartheid
1996	Adoption of the new constitution of South Africa
2013	Death of Nelson Mandela
2018	The worst drought the country has faced in over 100 years

THE AUTHORS

ANNA MAKANDA

Anna was born in Gweru, Zimbabwe, and raised in London, along with her older sister. Her father is Zimbabwean and her mother, Scottish. Growing up, Anna always dreamed of owning her own business. She started her career as an accountant but soon realized it was time to pursue her dreams. Anna now has her own fitness business. In her spare time, you will find her working on one of her endless ideas or spending time with her family.

SHARMANE BARRETT

Sharmane was born and raised in London, along with her five sisters. Her father is Jamaican and her mother, Trinidadian-English. Growing up, Sharmane was encouraged to pursue a career as a lawyer but after completing her legal studies, she soon realized that law was not for her. She began working in legal recruitment, which gave her an opportunity to live in Singapore for almost four years. Sharmane's passions are travelling and boxing and; although these days there is a lot less travelling to exotic destinations, and a lot more time in the gym.

THE ILLUSTRATOR

ROSIE EDWARDS

Rosie was born in Wiltshire, England, where she grew up with her parents, older brother and family dogs. She has a degree in Textiles from Cardiff Metropolitan University and experience in designing homeware, stationery, and greetings collections, focusing on children's products. Rosie fell in love with the world building and story telling of children's books and knew this was the avenue she wanted to explore. Based now in Northern Ireland, Rosie loves to travel. If she wasn't an artist she'd like to be cabin crew for a long-haul airline. Luckily, being a freelance illustrator gives her the same freedom, just sadly without the fabulous uniform.

OUR GRATITUDE

We would like to say thank you and extend our gratitude to:

Everyone who helped us with the research; Caitlin Bookless and Martin Mwamoni, for your advice, opinions, and, most importantly, time. Thank you.

Our editor, Amber, our proof-reader, Adam, and Martyn, our wonderful designer, who not only made our books look as beautiful as they do but also helped us articulate our vision so perfectly. To our illustrator, Rosie, for bringing Lerato, Kaya and Thabo to life, and for showcasing the magic of South Africa.

And not forgetting all our little people for helping us pick the designs and road-testing the content.

Each other. This is a passion project for us both and to be able to share this journey with a best friend is the dream.

Anna and Sharmane

LET'S EXPLORE MORE

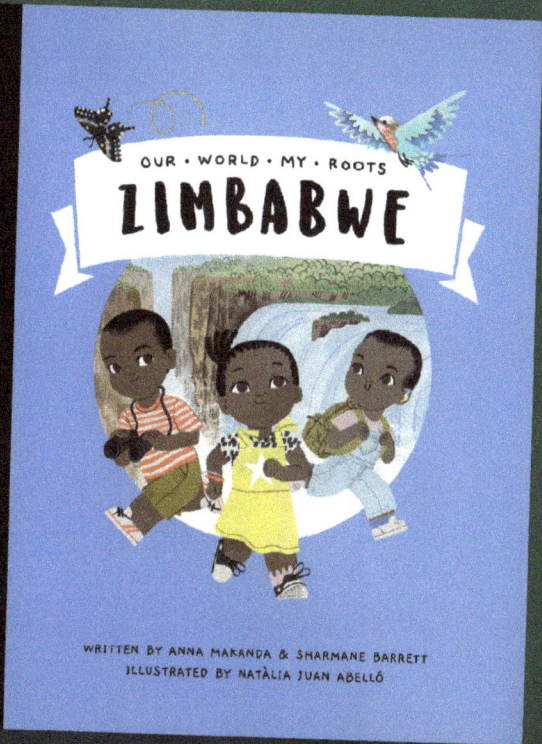

OUR · WORLD · MY · ROOTS
ZIMBABWE

WRITTEN BY ANNA MAKANDA & SHARMANE BARRETT
ILLUSTRATED BY NATÀLIA JUAN ABELLÓ

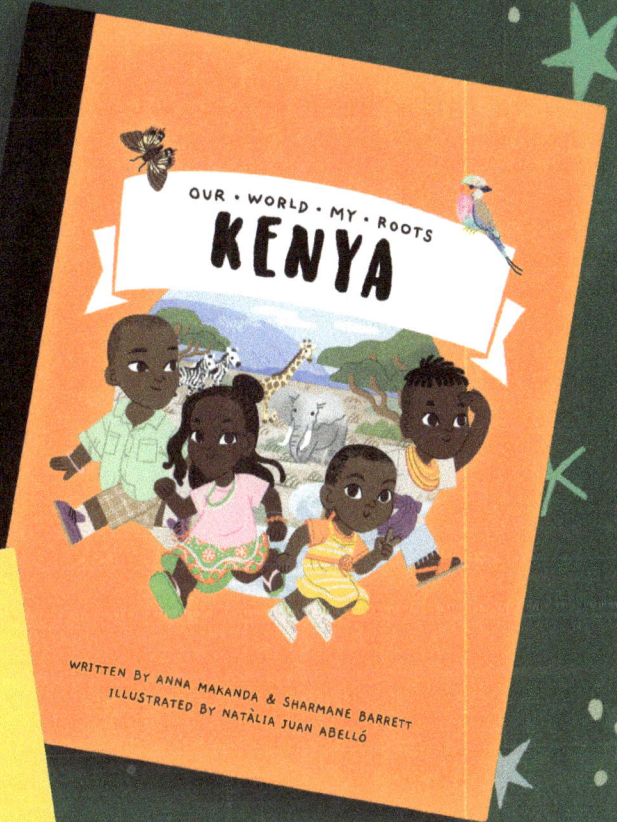

OUR · WORLD · MY · ROOTS
KENYA

WRITTEN BY ANNA MAKANDA & SHARMANE BARRETT
ILLUSTRATED BY NATÀLIA JUAN ABELLÓ

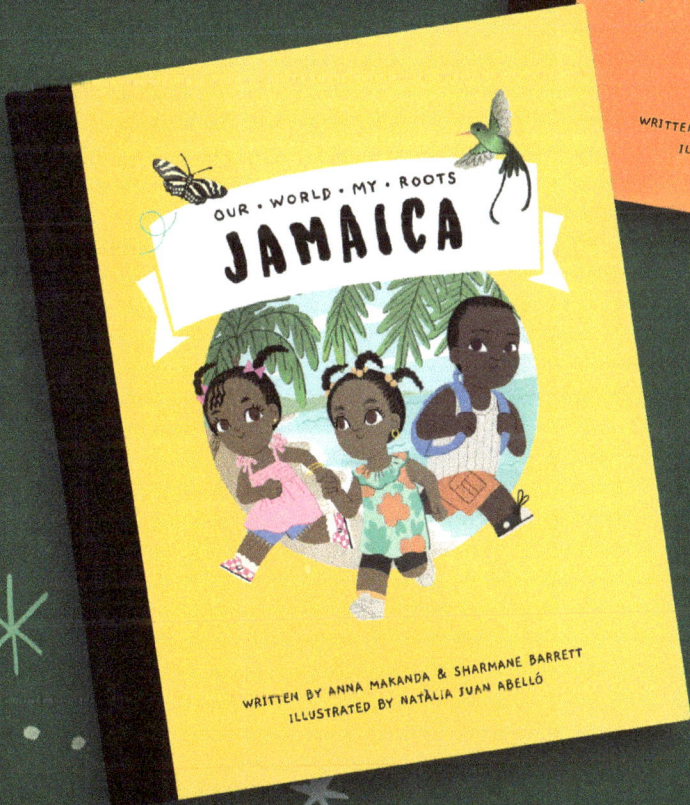

OUR · WORLD · MY · ROOTS
JAMAICA

WRITTEN BY ANNA MAKANDA & SHARMANE BARRETT
ILLUSTRATED BY NATÀLIA JUAN ABELLÓ

OUR MISSION

Our mission is to help ignite a child's interest in their roots and empower them to become culturally confident. We aim to do this by providing parents and caregivers factual yet engaging resources to help them teach their children about their culture and heritage.

COPYRIGHT

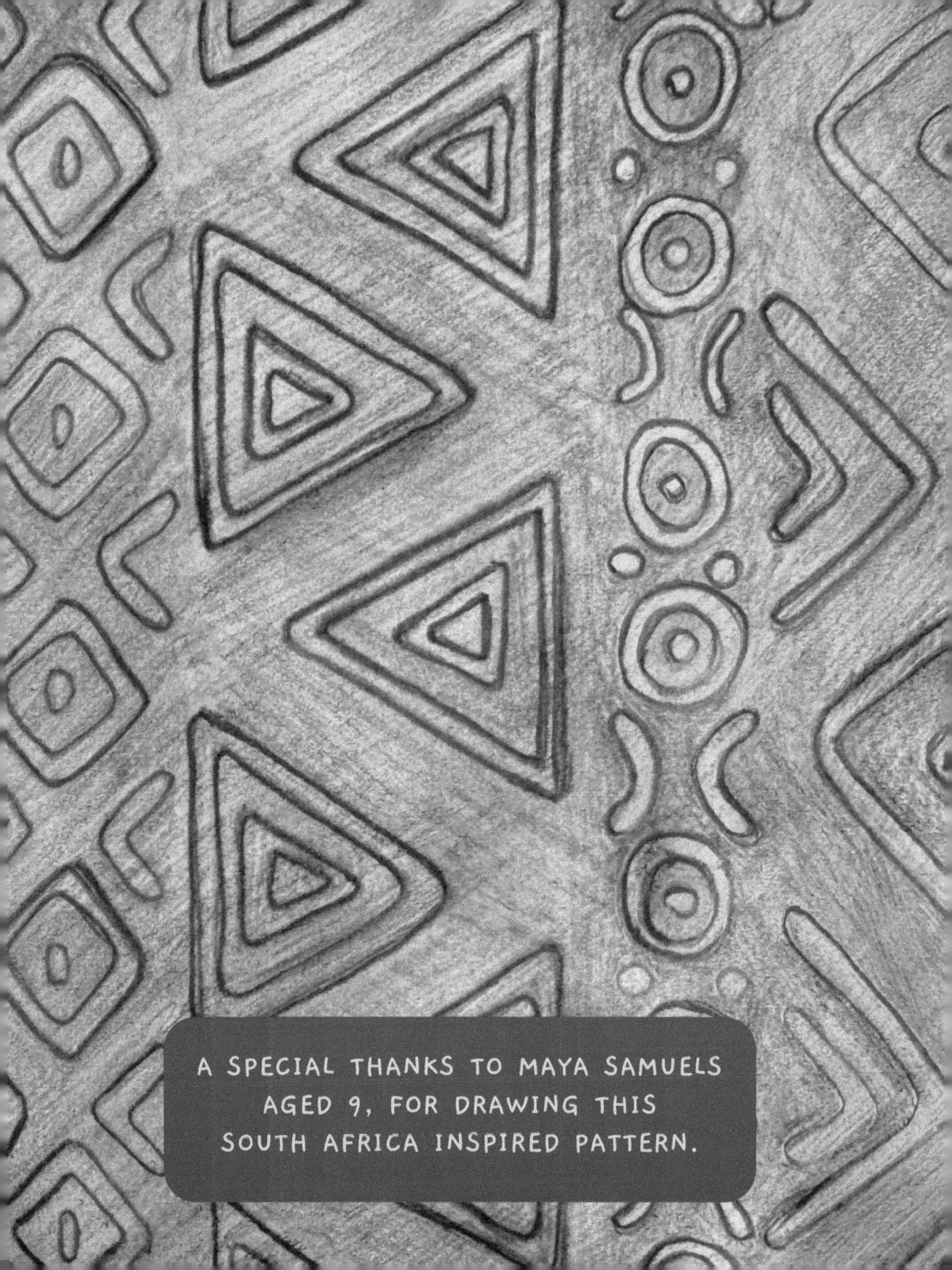

A SPECIAL THANKS TO MAYA SAMUELS
AGED 9, FOR DRAWING THIS
SOUTH AFRICA INSPIRED PATTERN.

www.ingramcontent.com/pod-product-compliance
Lightning Source LLC
Chambersburg PA
CBHW060803150426
42813CB00059B/2866

* 9 7 8 1 0 6 8 6 4 3 9 1 0 *